Dolch
Sight Word Activities

By Carol Marinovich

Volume 1

Grand Rapids, MI

Edited by Linda Hartley
Designed by Vicki Langeliers
Illustrated by Larry Brown

Frank Schaffer Publications®

Send all inquiries to:
Frank Schaffer Publications
3195 Wilson Drive NW
Grand Rapids, Michigan 49534

ISBN 1-56189-917-8

7 8 9 10 11 12 VHG 09 08 07 06 05

Dolch
Sight Word Activities
Volume 1

Purpose

Dolch Sight Word Activities, Volumes 1 and 2 provide a systematic and sequential method for teaching children the 220 Dolch basic sight words that are needed for a successful experience in beginning reading. *Volume 1* covers 110 of the words in the list and *Volume 2* covers the rest of the words in the list.

The lessons provided in these volumes are designed for quality parent/teacher-student interaction. It is important that you preview with the children the words to be learned prior to the written assignment. This will insure that the children will recognize each word that they are reading and writing.

Each unit introduces a set of five words from the Dolch Sight Words list. The words are presented and reviewed in a consistent way.

Each unit consists of six lessons. The first lesson in the unit introduces the five words by allowing children to trace over the letters. The second lesson allows the children to match words beginning with upper-case letters to the same words beginning with lower-case letters and also to read sentences containing the new words, then draw pictures about the sentences to demonstrate comprehension. The third lesson focuses on recognizing the letters in the words. In the fourth lesson, the children fill in the letters that are missing in the words. In the fifth lesson, children practice sentence completion skills, and the sixth lesson provides children with the opportunity to utilize the new words that they have learned in a meaningful context. An award certificate is supplied at the end of the book. This award certificate provides positive student reinforcement at the completion of this workbook.

Vocabulary Selection

The *Dolch Sight Word Activities Workbooks* use the classic Dolch list of 220 basic vocabulary words that make up from 50% to 75% of all reading matter that children ordinarily encounter. Since these words are ordinarily recognized on sight, they are called *sight words*. *Volume 1* includes 110 sight words. *Volume 2* covers the remainder of the list. Since very few nouns are included in the Dolch list of 220 basic vocabulary words, certain nouns from the Dolch 95 Common Nouns List are added to provide a more meaningful context.

Lesson Instructions

Letter Tracing

Point to the first word in dark print. Read the word to the child and spell the word, pointing to each letter as you say it. Then repeat the word. Finally, have the child trace over the word with a pencil.

If the word is in a sentence, read the sentence to the child. Have the child repeat the sentence. Then ask the child to read the word again. Have the child say each letter in the word as you point to it. Then have the child trace over the word.

Praise the child if the word and letters are said correctly. If a child has difficulty, repeat the activity until the child can read the word.

Repeat this procedure for each of the next four words. Finish the lesson by reviewing all of the words introduced in the worksheet. Do this by pointing at random to each word and asking the child to read the word.

Matching and Visualization

Have the child draw a line to match each word beginning with an upper-case letter to the same word beginning with a lower-case letter.

Then ask the child to read the first sentence over the box aloud. Talk with the child about a picture that could go with that sentence. Using crayons, have the child draw a picture that shows what the sentence is about.

Continue this procedure with the other sentence. When the child has finished drawing, have the child reread both sentences and tell about the pictures.

Scrambled Words

Ask the child to read the first word on the page. Then have the child think of a sentence using that word. Have the child copy the word on the line beside it.

To reinforce the letters that make up the word and to review alphabetical skills, have the child cut out the letters at the bottom of the page and match the letters to the letters in the word being studied. The child can then glue the word onto this line over the printed letters.

Repeat this procedure for the other words on the worksheet unless you find that the child can do the activity independently. If this is the case, have the child read the words aloud to you after completion of the page.

If you wish, you can have the child simply copy the words on the lines instead of cutting them out.

Missing Letters

Point to the word at the top of each section and have the child repeat it after you. If a child has difficulty reading the words, review the words with the child individually.

Then ask the child to write the missing letters for each of the words.

Sentence Completion

If the child is still experiencing difficulty in remembering any of the words, review the words prior to the written work. Use the procedures described in the preceding lessons.

Tell the child to read the words in the box and then read each incomplete sentence. Ask the child to find the word from the box that makes each sentence complete and write it in the blank.

Then ask the child to read the sentences aloud.

Oral Reading/Parent Participation

Tell the child to read the new words in sentences. Then ask the child to read the sentences aloud. Pronounce any words that the child has trouble with.

Student Award

Present the child with an award certificate upon completion of the workbook. The award certificate is located at the end of this book.

The child can color the certificate and display it.

Dolch Sight Word Activities

Name _____

Directions: Tell the children, "Read the word that goes with each picture. Then say its letters. Repeat the word. Now trace the word with your pencil."

can

girl

boy

read

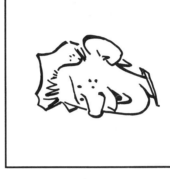

can

girl

boy

read

Directions: Tell the children, "Read the sentence below. Say the new word printed in dark print. Then say its letters. Repeat the word. Now trace the word with your pencil."

Can **a** boy read?

Name

Directions: Tell the children, "Draw a line from each word that begins with a capital letter to the same word that begins with a small letter."

Boy   girl

A   can

Read   boy

Girl   read

Can   a

A boy can read.

A girl can read.

Directions: Tell the children, "Read each sentence. Draw a picture that shows what the sentence means."

Dolch **Sight Word Activities**

Name _____

can _____

boy _____

read _____

a _____

girl _____

a	a	a	b	c	d	e	g	i	l	l	n	o	r	r	y

Directions: Tell the children, "Copy each of the words on the line next to the word."

Optional Activity: Tell the children, "Cut out the letters at the bottom of the page. Use the letters to make the words. Then glue each word on the line beside the printed word."

Dolch **Sight Word Activities**

Name _____

can

c _____ _____

_____ a _____

boy

_____ _____ y

b _____ _____

read

r _____ _____ d

_____ e a _____

a

_____ _____ _____ _____

girl

_____ _____ r l

_____ i r _____

Dalch **Sight Word Activities**

Name _____

a
can
girl
read
boy

1. Can _____ _ _ _ _ boy read?

2. Can a girl _____ _ _ _ _ ?

3. A boy _____ _ _ _ _ read.

4. A _____ _ _ _ _ can read.

5. Can a _____ _ _ _ _ read?

Directions: Tell the children, "Read the words in dark print. Then read the incomplete sentences. Find the word in dark print that correctly completes each sentence. Then write that word in the blank."

Dolch Sight Word Activities

Name _____

PARENTS: Listen to your child read the sentences on this page and put a check mark beside each sentence that is read **without** error. Then display the paper in a prominent place. If your child has difficulty with any sentence, read the sentence to the child, pointing to each word as you read. Ask the child to read the sentence in the same way. Repeat this procedure several times.

☐ A girl can read.

☐ A boy can read.

☐ Can a girl read?

☐ A girl read.

☐ Can a boy read?

☐ A boy read.

Directions: Tell the children, "Learn to read the sentences, then take them home to read to your parents. Notice that the word **read** can be pronounced both /rēd/ and /rĕd/."

Dolch **Sight Word Activities**

Name _____

Directions: Tell the children, "Read the word that goes with each picture. Then say its letters. Repeat the word. Now trace the word with your pencil."

book

book

sing

sing

puppy

puppy

cat

cat

Directions: Tell the children, "Read the sentence below. Say the new word printed in dark print. Then say its letters. Repeat the word. Now trace the word with your pencil."

A cat can **not** sing. not

Dolch Sight Word Activities

Name _____

Directions: Tell the children, "Draw a line from each word that begins with a capital letter to the same word that begins with a small letter."

Sing   book

Not   puppy

Cat   sing

Puppy   not

Book   cat

Can a puppy read a book?

A girl can sing.

Directions: Tell the children, "Read each sentence. Draw a picture that shows what the sentence means."

Dolch **Sight Word Activities**

Name _____

puppy _____   cat _____

not _____   book _____

sing _____

a	b	c	g	i	k	n	n	o	o	o
p	p	p	s	t	t	u	y			

Directions: Tell the children, "Copy each of the words on the line next to the word."

Optional Activity: Tell the children, "Cut out the letters at the bottom of the page. Use the letters to make the words. Then glue each word on the line beside the printed word."

Dolch **Sight Word Activities**

Name _____

puppy

__ __ __ p p y

p u __ __ y

cat

__ __ __ t

c __ __

not

__ __ n

__ __ o

book

b __ __ k

__ __ o o

sing

__ __ i __ g

__ __ in __

Dolch Sight Word Activities

Name _____

puppy
cat
not
book
sing

1. Can a _ _ _ _ _ _ _ _ read?

2. Can a puppy _ _ _ _ _ _ _ ?

3. Can a cat read a _ _ _ _ _ _ ?

4. A puppy can _ _ _ _ _ _ _ sing.

5. A _ _ _ _ _ _ _ can not sing.

Directions: Tell the children, "Read the words in dark print. Then read the incomplete sentences. Find the word in dark print that correctly completes each sentence. Then write that word in the blank."

Dolch **Sight Word Activities**

Name _____

PARENTS: Listen to your child read the sentences on this page and put a check mark beside each sentence that is read without error. Then display the paper in a prominent place. If your child has difficulty with any sentence, read the sentence to the child, pointing to each word as you read. Ask the child to read the sentence in the same way. Repeat this procedure several times.

☐ A girl can read a book.

☐ A puppy can not read a book.

☐ A girl can sing.

☐ A boy can sing.

☐ Can a cat sing?

☐ A puppy can not sing.

Directions: Tell the children, "Learn to read the sentences, then take them home to read to your parents."

Dolch Sight Word Activities

Name _____

Directions: Tell the children, "Read the word that goes with each picture. Then say its letters. Repeat the word. Now trace the word with your pencil."

run

run

laugh

laugh

jump

jump

Directions: Tell the children, "Read each sentence below. Say the new word printed in dark print. Then say its letters. Repeat the word. Now trace the word with your pencil."

A boy **had** a book.   had

A puppy **and** a girl can run.   and

Name _____

Directions: Tell the children, "Draw a line from each word that begins with a capital letter to the same word that begins with a small letter."

And

Had

Jump

Laugh

Run

laugh

run

and

had

jump

A girl can jump.

A puppy can run.

Directions: Tell the children, "Read each sentence. Draw a picture that shows what the sentence means."

Dolch **Sight Word Activities**

Name _____

_____ jump

_____ run

_____ and

_____ laugh

_____ had

a	a	a	d	d	g	h	h	j
l	l	m	n	n	p	r	u	u	u

Directions: Tell the children, "Copy each of the words on the line next to the word."

Optional Activity: Tell the children, "Cut out the letters at the bottom of the page. Use the letters to make the words. Then glue each word on the line beside the printed word."

Dolch **Sight Word Activities**

Name _____

had

h _ _

_ _ a

jump

_ u _ p

j _ m _

laugh

l _ _ ug

_ a _ gh

run

r _ d

_ _ n

and

_ _ d

_ _ n

Directions: Tell the children, "Say each word printed in dark type. Fill in the missing letters."

Dolch Sight Word Activities

Name _____

laugh
run
jump
and
had

1. A cat can not _____ _ _ _ _ _ _ .

2. A boy _____ a book.

3. A boy _____ girl can read a book.

4. Can a puppy _____ _ _ _ _ _ _ ?

5. Can a cat _____ _ _ _ _ _ _ ?

Directions: Tell the children, "Read the words in dark print. Then read the incomplete sentences. Find the word in dark print that correctly completes each sentence. Then write that word in the blank."

Dolch **Sight Word Activities**

Name _____

PARENTS: Listen to your child read the sentences on this page and put a check mark beside each sentence that is read without error. Then display the paper in a prominent place. If your child has difficulty with any sentence, read the sentence to the child, pointing to each word as you read. Ask the child to read the sentence in the same way. Repeat this procedure several times.

☐ A cat and a puppy can jump and run.

☐ A girl had a puppy and a cat.

☐ Can a cat and a puppy sing and laugh?

☐ A boy can read, and a girl can read.

☐ A puppy and a cat can not read.

☐ A puppy and a boy can run.

Directions: Tell the children, "Learn to read the sentences, then take them home to read to your parents."

Dolch **Sight Word Activities**

Name _____

Directions: Tell the children, "Read each sentence below. Say the new word printed in dark print. Then say its letters. Repeat the word. Now trace the word with your pencil. Notice that the word **read** can be pronounced two ways: /rēd/ and /rĕd/."

A puppy **with** a book can not read.　　**with**

A boy can read **the** book.　　**the**

The girl read a **funny** book.　　**funny**

The puppy **is** funny.　　**is**

The boy can run **fast**.　　**fast**

Dolch **Sight Word Activities**

Name _____

Directions: Tell the children, "Draw a line from each word that begins with a capital letter to the same word that begins with a small letter."

With

The

Is

Funny

Fast

the

funny

with

fast

is

The boy with the puppy can sing.

The girl and the cat can run fast.

Directions: Tell the children, "Read each sentence. Draw a picture that shows what the sentence means."

Dolch Sight Word Activities

Name _____

_____ with

_____ is

_____ funny

_____ the

_____ fast

a	e	f	f	h	h	i	i	n
n	s	s	t	t	t	u	w	y

Directions: Tell the children, "Copy each of the words on the line next to the word."

Optional Activity: Tell the children, "Cut out the letters at the bottom of the page. Use the letters to make the words. Then glue each word on the line beside the printed word."

Dolch **Sight Word Activities**

Name _____

funny

f _____ ny

_____ unn _____

with

_____ th

wi _____

the

_____ t

_____ h

fast

f _____ t

_____ as _____

is

_____ _____ _____

Directions: Tell the children, "Say each word printed in dark type. Fill in the missing letters."

Dolch **Sight Word Activities**

Name _____

the
with
funny
is
fast

1. _____ _ _ _ _ _ the puppy funny?

2. _____ _ _ _ _ _ cat can not laugh.

3. The boy can run _____ _ _ _ _ _ .

4. The book is _____ _ _ _ _ _ .

5. The girl read the book _____ _ _ _ _ _ the boy.

Directions: Tell the children, "Read the words in dark print. Then read the incomplete sentences. Find the word in dark print that correctly completes each sentence. Then write that word in the blank. Use a capital letter at the beginning of a sentence."

Dolch **Sight Word Activities**

Name _____

PARENTS: Listen to your child read the sentences on this page and put a check mark beside each sentence that is read without error. Then display the paper in a prominent place. If your child has difficulty with any sentence, read the sentence to the child, pointing to each word as you read. Ask the child to read the sentence in the same way. Repeat this procedure several times.

The puppy can
run fast with the girl.

The book is not
with the boy.

A cat is funny, and
a puppy is funny.

The girl had
a funny laugh.

The girl can read
the book fast.

The funny puppy
can run fast.

Directions: Tell the children, "Learn to read the sentences, then take them home to read to your parents."

Dolch **Sight Word Activities**

Name _____

Directions: Read the word that goes with each picture. Then say its letters. Repeat the word. Now trace the word with your pencil.

chair

grass

rain

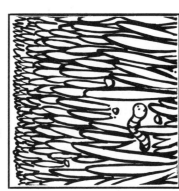

school

chair

grass

rain

school

Directions: Tell the children, "Read the sentence below. Say the new word printed in dark print. Then say its letters. Repeat the word. Now trace the word with your pencil."

The boy in the book had a puppy.   in

Dolch **Sight Word Activities**

Name _____

Directions: Tell the children, "Draw a line from each word that begins with a capital letter to the same word that begins with a small letter."

The girl is
in school.

The cat is in
a chair.

Directions: Tell the children, "Read each sentence. Draw a picture that shows what the sentence means."

In   school

Chair   grass

Grass   in

Rain   chair

School   rain

Dolch **Sight Word Activities**

Name _____

chair _____

_____ rain

school _____

_____ grass

in _____

a	a	a	c	c	g	h	h	h	i	i	i
l	n	n	o	o	r	r	r	s	s	s	s

Directions: Tell the children, "Copy each of the words on the line next to the word."

Optional Activity: Tell the children, "Cut out the letters at the bottom of the page. Use the letters to make the words. Then glue each word on the line beside the printed word."

Dalch **Sight Word Activities**

Name _____

in

___

___
---

chair

___ __air
---
cha__

grass

___ ra__s
---
g___ss

rain

__ai__
r___n

school

s__ho__l
__cho__l

Dolch Sight Word Activities

Name _____

grass
rain
school
chair
in

1. The girl read the book in _____ _ _ _ _ _ _ .

2. Can the puppy jump in the _____ _ _ _ _ _ _ ?

3. The girl is not in the _____ _ _ _ _ _ _ .

4. The cat is in the _____ _ _ _ _ _ _ .

5. The funny cat is _____ _ _ _ _ _ _ the chair with a book.

Directions: Tell the children, "Read the words in dark print. Then read the incomplete sentences. Find the word in dark print that correctly completes each sentence. Then write that word in the blank."

Dalch **Sight Word Activities**

Name _____

PARENTS: Listen to your child read the sentences on this page and put a check mark beside each sentence that is read without error. Then display the paper in a prominent place. If your child has difficulty with any sentence, read the sentence to the child, pointing to each word as you read. Ask the child to read the sentence in the same way. Repeat this procedure several times.

☐ The boy can read
in the chair.

☐ The girl can sing
in the rain.

☐ The boy can read the
funny book and laugh.

☐ The cat can not
run fast in the rain.

☐ Can a funny cat read
a book in school?

☐ The puppy can jump
and run in the grass.

Directions: Tell the children, "Learn to read the sentences, then take them home to read to your parents."

Dolch Sight Word Activities

Name _____

Directions: Tell the children, "Read each sentence below. Say the new word printed in dark print. Then say its letters. Repeat the word. Now trace the word with your pencil."

The boy **at** school can read. at

The puppy **will** jump and run. will

Will the girl **sit** in the chair? sit

Can a girl read **to** a cat? to

Is the puppy **on** the grass? on

Dolch **Sight Word Activities**

Name _____

Directions: Tell the children, "Draw a line from each word that begins with a capital letter to the same word that begins with a small letter."

At

Will

To

Sit

On

will

on

at

to

sit

The puppy can sit
on the chair.

The puppy can sit
on the grass.

Directions: Tell the children, "Read each sentence. Draw a picture that shows what the sentence means."

Dolch **Sight Word Activities**

Name _____

will _____

at _____

on _____

sit _____

to _____

a	i	i	l	l	n	o	o	s	t	t	t	w

Directions: Tell the children, "Copy each of the words on the line next to the word."

Optional Activity: Tell the children, "Cut out the letters at the bottom of the page. Use the letters to make the words. Then glue each word on the line beside the printed word."

Dolch **Sight Word Activities**

Name _____

to

___ ___ ___ ___ ___ ___

on

___ ___ ___ ___

will

___ i l ___

w ___ l ___

at

___ ___ ___ ___

sit

S ___ ___

___ i ___

Directions: Tell the children, "Say each word printed in dark type. Fill in the missing letters."

Dolch **Sight Word Activities**

Name _____

sit
to
will
at
on

1. _____ the puppy jump on the chair?

2. The book is _____ school.

3. The boy can _____ and read the book.

4. The girl will sing _____ the boy.

5. Can the cat sit _____ the grass?

Directions: Tell the children, "Read the words in dark print. Then read the incomplete sentences. Find the word in dark print that correctly completes each sentence. Then write that word in the blank. Use a capital letter at the beginning of a sentence."

Dolch Sight Word Activities

Name _____

PARENTS: Listen to your child read the sentences on this page and put a check mark beside each sentence that is read without error. Then display the paper in a prominent place. If your child has difficulty with any sentence, read the sentence to the child, pointing to each word as you read. Ask the child to read the sentence in the same way. Repeat this procedure several times.

☐ The girl will sit on the grass to read a funny book.

☐ The boy and girl had to run to school fast.

☐ The boy can sit on a chair with a puppy and sing.

☐ The fast cat will run to the girl in the rain.

☐ At school, the girl will not jump on the chair.

☐ The boy will laugh at the funny puppy.

Directions: Tell the children, "Learn to read the sentences, then take them home to read to your parents."

Dalch Sight Word Activities

Name _____

Directions: Tell the children, "Read the word that goes with each picture. Then say its letters. Repeat the word. Now trace the word with your pencil."

play

play

ball

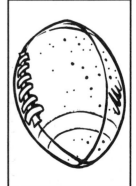

ball

Directions: Tell the children, "Read each sentence below. Say the new word printed in dark print. Then say its letters. Repeat the word. Now trace the word with your pencil."

A girl can **go** to school.   **go**

I can play with the puppy.   **I**

The cat in the grass is **brown**.   **brown**

Dalch Sight Word Activities

Name _____

Directions: Tell the children, "Draw a line from each word that begins with a capital letter to the same word that begins with a small letter. Point out to the children that the word *I* is never written with a small letter."

Go

Play

Ball

Brown

ball

brown

play

go

The girl can play
ball with the boy.

The brown ball is
on the chair.

Directions: Tell the children, "Read each sentence. Draw a picture that shows what the sentence means."

Dolch Sight Word Activities

Name _____

Unit 7
Scrambled Words 3

go _____

brown _____

play _____

ball _____

I _____

a	a	b	b	g	I	I	l
n	o	o	p	r	w	y	

Directions: Tell the children, "Copy each of the words on the line next to the word."

Optional Activity: Tell the children, "Cut out the letters at the bottom of the page. Use the letters to make the words. Then glue each word on the line beside the printed word."

Dolch **Sight Word Activities**

Name _____

play

p l _____

_____ a y

go

_____ _____ _____ _____

I

_____ _____ _____ _____

ball

_____ a l _____

b _____ l

brown

b _____ w n

_____ r o w _____

Name _____

go
ball
brown
play
I

1. The puppy can play with the _____ ------ .

2. _____ had to go to school in the rain.

3. The grass is not _____ ------ .

4. The girl and I can _____ ------ and sing.

5. Will the boy _____ ------ to school fast?

Directions: Tell the children, "Read the words in dark print. Then read the incomplete sentences. Find the word in dark print that correctly completes each sentence. Then write that word in the blank. Use a capital letter at the beginning of a sentence."

Dolch **Sight Word Activities**

Name _____

PARENTS: Listen to your child read the sentences on this page and put a check mark beside each sentence that is read without error. Then display the paper in a prominent place. If your child has difficulty with any sentence, read the sentence to the child, pointing to each word as you read. Ask the child to read the sentence in the same way. Repeat this procedure several times.

☐ I can go play ball
with a boy at school.

☐ A brown ball is
on the chair.

☐ I can laugh and play
with the funny puppy.

☐ The brown cat can run
fast with the ball.

☐ Can I read the brown
book in the rain?

☐ The cat and I will go sit
on the grass to play.

Directions: Tell the children, "Learn to read the sentences, then take them home to read to your parents."

Dolch **Sight Word Activities**

Name _____

Directions: Tell the children, "Read each sentence below. Say the new word printed in dark print. Then say its letters. Repeat the word. Now trace the word with your pencil."

Directions: Tell the children, "Read the word that goes with each picture. Then say its letters. Repeat the word. Now trace the word with your pencil."

house

house

saw

saw

I will **look** at the funny house.

look

The **little** puppy can run fast.

little

I will read a book **today.**

today

Dalch Sight Word Activities

Name _____

Directions: Tell the children, "Draw a line from each word that begins with a capital letter to the same word that begins with a small letter."

House

Look

Little

Saw

Today

look

today

house

little

saw

The saw is little.

The house is not little.

Directions: Tell the children, "Read each sentence. Draw a picture that shows what the sentence means."

Dolch **Sight Word Activities**

Name _____

little _____

look _____

saw _____

house _____

today _____

a	a	e	e	h	i	k	l	l	o	o
o	o	s	s	t	t	t	u	w	y	

Directions: Tell the children, "Copy each of the words on the line next to the word."

Optional Activity: Tell the children, "Cut out the letters at the bottom of the page. Use the letters to make the words. Then glue each word on line beside the printed word."

Dolch **Sight Word Activities**

Name _____

house

h __ __ se

__ ous __

look

__ oo __

l __ __ k

little

li __ __ le

__ ittl __

saw

__ __ a

s __ __

today

t __ __ ay

__ od __ y

Directions: Tell the children, "Say each word printed in dark type. Fill in the missing letters."

Dolch **Sight Word Activities**

Name _____

today
house
look
little
saw

1. The boy will not play in the _____ _____.

2. _____ I saw a funny little puppy.

3. Look at the cat sit in the _____ chair.

4. The girl will go in the house to _____ at the book.

5. I _____ a brown puppy play with the ball.

Directions: Tell the children, "Read the words in dark print. Then read the incomplete sentences. Find the word in dark print that correctly completes each sentence. Then write that word in the blank. Use a capital letter at the beginning of a sentence."

Dalch **Sight Word Activities**

Name _____

☐ Today I saw
a little house.

☐ I will look for
the brown ball today.

☐ Look! A cat and a
puppy can play with
a brown ball.

☐ The little puppy saw
a cat jump in the rain.

☐ A girl and a boy can sit
in the house and read.

☐ The boy saw a little cat
in the house today.

Directions: Tell the children, "Learn to read the sentences, then take them home to read to your parents."

Name _____

Directions: Tell the children, "Read the word that goes with the picture. Then say its letters. Repeat the word. Now trace the word with your pencil."

Directions: Tell the children, "Read each sentence below. Say the new word printed in dark print. Then say its letters. Repeat the word. Now trace the word with your pencil."

Is **it** funny?   it

The boy **does** run fast.   does

The cat is **white**.   white

The boy and the cat **are** funny.   are

monkey

monkey

Name _____

Directions: Tell the children, "Draw a line from each word that begins with a capital letter to the same word that begins with a small letter."

It

Does

Are

Monkey

White

monkey

it

white

does

are

The monkey is in the chair.

The monkey is in the rain.

Directions: Tell the children, "Read each sentence. Draw a picture that shows what the sentence means."

Dolch **Sight Word Activities**

Name _____

_____ _____

monkey _____ are _____

_ _ _ _ _ _ _ _ _ _ _ _ _ _ _ _ _ _ _ _

it _____ does _____

_ _ _ _ _ _ _ _ _ _ _ _ _ _ _ _ _ _ _ _

white _____

a	d	e	e	e	e	h	i	i	k	m
n	o	o	r	s	t	t	w	y		

Directions: Tell the children, "Copy each of the words on the line next to the word."

Optional Activity: Tell the children, "Cut out the letters at the bottom of the page. Use the letters to make the words. Then glue each word on the line beside the printed word."

Dolch Sight Word Activities

Name _____

it

_____ _ _ _ _ _

are

_____ _ _ _ _ e

_____ a

does

d _ _ _ _ s

_ _ _ oe

white

_____ _____

_ _ _ hit

w _ _ i _ e

monkey

m _ _ n _ _ ey

_ _ o _ key

Directions: Tell the children, "Say each word printed in dark type. Fill in the missing letters."

Dolch **Sight Word Activities**

Name _____

monkey
white
does
are
it

1. _____ the little puppy run fast? _____

2. The house the girl and I saw is _____

3. Will _____ rain today?

4. Look at the _____. It is funny.

5. The book and ball _____ brown.

Directions: Tell the children, "Read the words in dark print. Then read the incomplete sentences. Find the word in dark print that correctly completes each sentence. Then write that word in the blank. Use a capital letter at the beginning of a sentence."

Dolch **Sight Word Activities**

Name _____

PARENTS: Listen to your child read the sentences on this page and put a check mark beside each sentence that is read without error. Then display the paper in a prominent place. If your child has difficulty with any sentence, read the sentence to the child, pointing to each word as you read. Ask the child to read the sentence in the same way. Repeat this procedure several times.

☐ Does the monkey jump
and run on the grass?

☐ Will it rain
at school today?

☐ Does the white puppy
play with the ball?

☐ The white cat will not sit
on the chair.

☐ The monkey and the
puppy are funny.

☐ Are the boy and girl
fast with the ball?

Directions: Tell the children, "Learn to read the sentences, then take them home to read to your parents."

Dolch Sight Word Activities

Name _____

Directions: Tell the children, "Read each sentence below. Say the new word printed in dark print. Then say its letters. Repeat the word. Now trace the word with your pencil."

Does **he** play fast ball?

he

I **like** the funny monkey.

like

Can the girl **keep** the puppy?

keep

Can I **bring** the brown ball to school today?

bring

The white puppy is **for** the boy.

for

Dolch **Sight Word Activities**

Name _____

Directions: Tell the children, "Draw a line from each word that begins with a capital letter to the same word that begins with a small letter."

He

Keep

Like

Bring

For

bring

like

he

for

keep

The monkey can bring the brown ball to the girl.

The book is for the boy to keep.

Dolch **Sight Word Activities**

Name _____

_____

_____
for

_____
bring

_____
like

_____
keep

_____
he

b	e	e	e	e	f	g	h	i
i	k	k	l	l	n	o	p	r	r

Directions: Tell the children, "Copy each of the words on the line next to the word."

Optional Activity: Tell the children, "Cut out the letters at the bottom of the page. Use the letters to make the words. Then glue each word on the line beside the printed word."

Dolch Sight Word Activities

Name _____

he

_ _ _ _

keep

k _ _ p

_ ee _

like

_ i _ e

l _ _ k

bring

_ _ ing

br _ n _

for

f _ _

_ _ r

Directions: Tell the children, "Say each word printed in dark type. Fill in the missing letters."

Dalch **Sight Word Activities**

Name _____

like
keep
bring
for
he

1. _____ the white ball to school.

2. I had to _____ the cat in the house.

3. I _____ to sit and read a book.

4. Does _____ like to sing and play?

5. The little house is _____ the puppy.

Directions: Tell the children, "Read the words in dark print. Then read the incomplete sentences. Find the word in dark print that correctly completes each sentence. Then write that word in the blank. Use a capital letter at the beginning of a sentence."

Dolch **Sight Word Activities**

Name _____

PARENTS: Listen to your child read the sentences on this page and put a check mark beside each sentence that is read without error. Then display the paper in a prominent place. If your child has difficulty with any sentence, read the sentence to the child, pointing to each word as you read. Ask the child to read the sentence in the same way. Repeat this procedure several times.

☐ He can not keep
the saw in the house.

☐ Does he bring the
white puppy to school?

☐ Look at the monkey
bring the ball to the boy.

☐ I like to play house
with the little girl.

☐ The boy will keep the
book he saw on the chair.

☐ The cat and the puppy
are on the grass.

Directions: Tell the children, "Learn to read the sentences, then take them home to read to your parents."

Dolch Sight Word Activities

Name _____

Directions: Tell the children, "Read each sentence below. Say the new word printed in dark print. Then say its letters. Repeat the word. Now trace the word with your pencil."

He can look at it with **me.**   me

Can I keep **my** book at school today?   my

Will **she** like the funny little monkey?   she

Look! **See** the puppy run and jump in the rain!   See

Can she **come** and see the play?   come

Dalch **Sight Word Activities**

Name _____

Directions: Tell the children, "Draw a line from each word that begins with a capital letter to the same word that begins with a small letter."

Me	she
My	come
She	see
Come	my
See	me

See me and
my puppy run
in the grass.

I will play and she
can sing with me.

Directions: Tell the children, "Read each sentence. Draw a picture that shows what the sentence means."

Dolch **Sight Word Activities**

Name _____

me _____

she _____

come _____

my _____

see _____

c	e	e	e	e	h	m	m	m	o	s	s	y

Directions: Tell the children, "Copy each of the words on the line next to the word."

Optional Activity: Tell the children, "Cut out the letters at the bottom of the page. Use the letters to make the words. Then glue each word on the line beside the printed word."

Dolch Sight Word Activities

Name _____

she

_____ h _____ e

my

_____ _____ _____

me

_____ _____ _____

see

_____ e _____

s _____

come

_____ me _____

co _____

Directions: Tell the children, "Say each word printed in dark type. Fill in the missing letters."

Dolch **Sight Word Activities**

Name _____

see
she
come
me
my

1. _____ _ _ _ _ and play ball with the boy.

2. _____ _ _ _ _ will keep the book for me.

3. Come see _____ _ _ _ _ today.

4. Can he _____ _ _ _ _ the funny little monkey jump?

5. It is for _____ _ _ _ _ little white puppy.

Directions: Tell the children, "Read the words in dark print. Then read the incomplete sentences. Find the word in dark print that correctly completes each sentence. Then write that word in the blank. Use a capital letter at the beginning of a sentence."

Dolch **Sight Word Activities**

Name _____

PARENTS: Listen to your child read the sentences on this page and put a check mark beside each sentence that is read without error. Then display the paper in a prominent place. If your child has difficulty with any sentence, read the sentence to the child, pointing to each word as you read. Ask the child to read the sentence in the same way. Repeat this procedure several times.

She can come
with me to play
with my brown ball.

He will like the play
she saw today.

Can she see me laugh?

Come to my house
with me.

Does she like to play
with my little puppy?

Bring my cat to me.
I like to play with it.

Directions: Tell the children, "Learn to read the sentences, then take them home to read to your parents."

Dolch Sight Word Activities

Name _____

Directions: Tell the children, "Read the word that goes with each picture. Then say its letters. Repeat the word. Now trace the word with your pencil."

Directions: Tell the children, "Read each sentence below. Say the new word printed in dark print. Then say its letters. Repeat the word. Now trace the word with your pencil."

He will **find** the puppy in the house.

find

Where can you play with me?

Where

You can **put** the book on the chair.

put

you

you

under

under

Dolch **Sight Word Activities**

Name _____

Directions: Tell the children, "Draw a line from each word that begins with a capital letter to the same word that begins with a small letter."

You

Find

Where

Under

Put

put

where

find

you

under

You are in a chair
with a puppy.

You can find a cat
in the grass.

Directions: Tell the children, "Read each sentence. Draw a picture that shows what the sentence means."

Dolch **Sight Word Activities**

Name _____

where _____

_____ under

you _____

_____ put

find _____

d	d	e	e	e	f	h	i	n	n	o
p	r	r	t	u	u	u	w	y		

Directions: Tell the children, "Copy each of the words on the line next to the word."

Optional Activity: Tell the children, "Cut out the letters at the bottom of the page. Use the letters to make the words. Then glue each word on the line beside the printed word."

Dolch Sight Word Activities

Name _____

you

__ __ u __

__ o __

find

f __ __ d

__ in __

where

__ __ wh __ r

__ ere

under

__ n __ er

und __ __ __

put

__ __ u __

__ __ t

Dolch **Sight Word Activities**

Name _____

put
you
find
where
under

1. See the cat? It is _____ _____ the chair.

2. _____ is my brown book?

3. I had to _____ _____ the cat for the little girl.

4. Can _____ bring the funny monkey to me?

5. _____ the puppy in the little white house.

Directions: Tell the children, "Read the words in dark print. Then read the incomplete sentences. Find the word in dark print that correctly completes each sentence. Then write that word in the blank. Use a capital letter at the beginning of a sentence."

Dalch Sight Word Activities

Name _____

PARENTS: Listen to your child read the sentences on this page and put a check mark beside each sentence that is read without error. Then display the paper in a prominent place. If your child has difficulty with any sentence, read the sentence to the child, pointing to each word as you read. Ask the child to read the sentence in the same way. Repeat this procedure several times.

☐ You will find the funny puppy under the chair.

☐ Can you see where the little ball is?

☐ Where can you put a little brown monkey?

☐ Can you find the little ball under the book?

☐ Put the book where you can find it.

☐ Can you put the brown monkey where it can see me?

Directions: Tell the children, "Learn to read the sentences, then take them home to read to your parents."

Dolch **Sight Word Activities**

Name _____

Directions: Tell the children, "Read each sentence below. Say the new word printed in dark print. Then say its letters. Repeat the word. Now trace the word with your pencil."

The boy **has** a white cat to play with.   has

Yes, the puppy will find the ball.   Yes

Where **did** the brown cat go today?   did

The boy and the girl are in a **big** house.   big

You and I can run to school **together**.   together

Dolch **Sight Word Activities**

Name _____

Directions: Tell the children, "Draw a line from each word that begins with a capital letter to the same word that begins with a small letter."

Has

Yes

Together

Did

Big

yes

big

did

has

together

You and the
brown monkey
play together.

You find a big cat
in the rain.

Directions: Tell the children, "Read each sentence. Draw a picture that shows what the sentence means."

Dolch **Sight Word Activities**

Name _____

together _____

yes _____

has _____

big _____

did _____

a	b	d	d	e	e	e	g	g	h
i	i	o	r	s	s	t	t	y	

Directions: Tell the children, "Copy each of the words on the line next to the word."

Optional Activity: Tell the children, "Cut out the letters at the bottom of the page. Use the letters to make the words. Then glue each word on the line beside the printed word."

Dolch **Sight Word Activities**

Name _____

has

h __ __

__ __ s

yes

__ e __

__ __ s

did

__ __ d

__ i __

big

b __ __

__ i __

together

to __ __ ther

togeth __ __

Dolch **Sight Word Activities**

Name _____

together
has
yes
did
big

1. My funny monkey _____ a brown ball.

2. The boy and I are in school _____ _____ .

3. _____ you see my white cat?

4. Does the chair look _____ to you?

5. _____ , you can play ball with me.

Directions: Tell the children, "Read the words in dark print. Then read the incomplete sentences. Find the word in dark print that correctly completes each sentence. Then write that word in the blank. Use a capital letter at the beginning of a sentence."

Dolch **Sight Word Activities**

Name _____

PARENTS: Listen to your child read the sentences on this page and put a check mark beside each sentence that is read without error. Then display the paper in a prominent place. If your child has difficulty with any sentence, read the sentence to the child, pointing to each word as you read. Ask the child to read the sentence in the same way. Repeat this procedure several times.

□ Yes, I can keep the big puppy in the house.

□ The girl has a monkey book at school.

□ Did you put the cat on my white chair?

□ She and I will read the big book she has.

□ I did not find the brown ball where you keep it.

□ The puppy and I like to run together in the grass.

Directions: Tell the children, "Learn to read the sentences, then take them home to read to your parents."

Dolch **Sight Word Activities**

Name _____

Directions: Tell the children, "Read the word that goes with the picture. Then say its letters. Repeat the word. Now trace the word with your pencil."

Directions: Tell the children, "Read each sentence below. Say the new word printed in dark print. Then say its letters. Repeat the word. Now trace the word with your pencil."

Will **your** mother come to school?

your

You can come **over** to my house.

over

I **went** to look for the monkey.

went

Do you **know** the little girl?

know

mother

mother

Dolch **Sight Word Activities**

Name _____

Directions: Tell the children, "Draw a line from each word that begins with a capital letter to the same word that begins with a small letter."

Mother   over

Your   went

Went   mother

Over   know

Know   your

My mother read me a book.

Your mother went to see you play ball.

Directions: Tell the children, "Read each sentence. Draw a picture that shows what the sentence means."

Dolch **Sight Word Activities**

Name _____

mother _____ ---- _____ know

over _____ ---- _____ went

your _____ ----

e	e	e	h	k	m	n	o	o	o
o	r	r	r	r	t	t	u	v	w	w	w	y

Directions: Tell the children, "Copy each of the words on the line next to the word."

Optional Activity: Tell the children, "Cut out the letters at the bottom of the page. Use the letters to make the words. Then glue each word on the line beside the printed word."

Dolch **Sight Word Activities**

Name _____

mother

mo __ __ er

__ __ ther

your

y __ __ r

__ __ ou __

went

__ __ en __

w __ __ __ t

over

ov __ __

__ __ er

know

__ n __ w

k __ __ o

Dalch Sight Word Activities

Name _____

went
mother
your
know
over

1. My _____ _____ will like to read the book.

2. The girl and I _____ _____ to school together.

3. Did _____ mother like my big cat?

4. The rain will be _____ today. It can not go on.

5. Does your mother _____ the little girl you like?

Directions: Tell the children, "Read the words in dark print. Then read the incomplete sentences. Find the word in dark print that correctly completes each sentence. Then write that word in the blank."

Name _____

PARENTS: Listen to your child read the sentences on this page and put a check mark beside each sentence that is read without error. Then display the paper in a prominent place. If your child has difficulty with any sentence, read the sentence to the child, pointing to each word as you read. Ask the child to read the sentence in the same way. Repeat this procedure several times.

☐ Did your mother go over to the school in the rain?

☐ Can she come over?

☐ The little monkey went over to play with the little girl.

☐ Your cat went to find the little puppy.

☐ I know my mother has a book for your mother.

☐ Does the little boy know where your house is?

Directions: Tell the children, "Learn to read the sentences, then take them home to read to your parents."

Dalch **Sight Word Activities**

Name _____

Directions: Tell the children, "Read the word that goes with the picture. Then say its letters. Repeat the word. Now trace the word with your pencil."

Directions: Tell the children, "Read each sentence below. Say the new word printed in dark print. Then say its letters. Repeat the word. Now trace the word with your pencil."

Do you know **how** to play ball?

how

How **do** you **do**?

do

Your father **was** at my school today.

was

Can **we** play with the white cat?

we

father

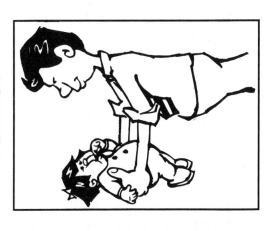

father

Dolch **Sight Word Activities**

Name _____

Directions: Tell the children, "Draw a line from each word that begins with a capital letter to the same word that begins with a small letter."

We

How

Do

Father

Was

do

father

we

was

how

I know how to play on a see saw.

Father and I put your book together.

Directions: Tell the children, "Read each sentence. Draw a picture that shows what the sentence means."

Dolch **Sight Word Activities**

Name _____

_____   was

_____   do

_____   father

_____   we

_____   how

a	a	d	e	e	f	h	h	o
o	r	s	t	w	w	w

Directions: Tell the children, "Copy each of the words on the line next to the word."

Optional Activity: Tell the children, "Cut out the letters at the bottom of the page. Use the letters to make the words. Then glue each word on the line beside the printed word."

Dolch **Sight Word Activities**

Name _____

we

_____ _____ _____

how

_____ o _____

h

do

_____ _____ _____ _____

father

fa _____ er

_____ ther

was

_____ _____ s

w _____

Dolch Sight Word Activities

Name _____

was
we
how
do
father

1. _____ ‿ ‿ ‿ _____ are you?

2. _____ _____ know how to sing.

3. _____ ‿ ‿ ‿ you know my father?

4. The puppy _____ ‿ ‿ ‿ over at my house.

5. _____ ‿ ‿ ‿ , can your little girl play in the rain?

Directions: Tell the children, "Read the words in dark print. Then read the incomplete sentences. Find the word in dark print that correctly completes each sentence. Then write that word in the blank. Use a capital letter at the beginning of a sentence."

Dolch **Sight Word Activities**

Name _____

PARENTS: Listen to your child read the sentences on this page and put a check mark beside each sentence that is read without error. Then display the paper in a prominent place. If your child has difficulty with any sentence, read the sentence to the child, pointing to each word as you read. Ask the child to read the sentence in the same way. Repeat this procedure several times.

☐ Father and I like to laugh at the funny cat.

☐ How was the school play?

☐ Do you know how to run fast?

☐ The ball was under the chair where we put it.

☐ Mother was with Father at the big white house.

☐ We went with your father to see the brown monkey.

Directions: Tell the children, "Learn to read the sentences, then take them home to read to your parents."

Dolch **Sight Word Activities**

Name _____

Directions: Tell the children, "Read the word that goes with the picture. Then say its letters. Repeat the word. Now trace the word with your pencil."

Directions: Tell the children, "Read each sentence below. Say the new word printed in dark print. Then say its letters. Repeat the word. Now trace the word with your pencil."

Is **this** book funny?

Can you **get** the little monkey?

get

Will you get **up** and play with me?

up

You can play with **our** big puppy.

our

cut

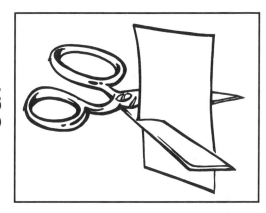

cut

Dolch **Sight Word Activities**

Name _____

Directions: Tell the children, "Draw a line from each word that begins with a capital letter to the same word that begins with a small letter."

This puppy can
sit with Mother
in the chair.

I will get a chair
for our father.

This	up
Get	cut
Up	our
Cut	get
Our	this

Directions: Tell the children, "Read each sentence. Draw a picture that shows what the sentence means."

Dolch **Sight Word Activities**

Name _____

this _____

our _____

cut _____

up _____

get _____

c	e	g	h	i	o	p	r	s	t	t	u	u	u

Directions: Tell the children, "Copy each of the words on the line next to the word."

Optional Activity: Tell the children, "Cut out the letters at the bottom of the page. Use the letters to make the words. Then glue each word on the line beside the printed word."

Dalch Sight Word Activities

Name _____

this

____ i s

t h ____

get

____ g ____

____ e

up

____

____

____

cut

____ t

c ____

our

____ u ____

____ o

Dolch Sight Word Activities

Name _____

our
cut
up
get
this

1. The boy has a _____ _____ .

2. Can you keep _____ _____ with me?

3. Where did you see _____ _____ cat?

4. Is _____ _____ the school where you went to play ball?

5. _____ _____ the book and bring it in the house.

Directions: Tell the children, "Read the words in dark print. Then read the incomplete sentences. Find the word in dark print that correctly completes each sentence. Then write that word in the blank. Use a capital letter at the beginning of a sentence."

Dolch Sight Word Activities

Name _____

PARENTS: Listen to your child read the sentences on this page and put a check mark beside each sentence that is read without error. Then display the paper in a prominent place. If your child has difficulty with any sentence, read the sentence to the child, pointing to each word as you read. Ask the child to read the sentence in the same way. Repeat this procedure several times.

☐ Get up and go
to school.

☐ Where did our father
go to school?

☐ Did you get the book
for your mother?

☐ We can not cut the
grass in the rain.

☐ This puppy is not
little; it is big.

☐ Yes, we can get
together at our house.

Directions: Tell the children, "Learn to read the sentences, then take them home to read to your parents."

Dolch **Sight Word Activities**

Name _____

Directions: Tell the children, "Read each sentence below. Say the new word printed in dark print. Then say its letters. Repeat the word. Now trace the word with your pencil."

Can we take the monkey with **us**? us

We will **all** go to school together. all

I will see you **after** school. after

School is **out**! out

How did your book get over **here**? here

Dolch **Sight Word Activities**

Name _____

Directions: Tell the children, "Draw a line from each word that begins with a capital letter to the same word that begins with a small letter."

A boy and a monkey can play together.

We all will play with the ball.

us

here

all

out

after

After

Out

Here

All

Us

Directions: Tell the children, "Read each sentence. Draw a picture that shows what the sentence means."

Dalch **Sight Word Activities**

Name _____

_____

all _____

_____

after _____

us _____

out _____

here _____

a	a	e	e	e	f	h	l
o	r	r	s	t	t	u	u

Directions: Tell the children, "Copy each of the words on the line next to the word."

Optional Activity: Tell the children, "Cut out the letters at the bottom of the page. Use the letters to make the words. Then glue each word on the line beside the printed word."

Dolch **Sight Word Activities**

Name _____

after

a ___ er

aft ___

out

___ u ___

___ ___ t

here

___ h ___ e

___ er ___

all

___ a ___

___ l ___

us

___ ___ ___

Directions: Tell the children, "Say each word printed in dark type. Fill in the missing letters."

Dalch Sight Word Activities

Name _____

all
here
after
us
out

1. _____ is our little puppy.

2. We will _____ play together.

3. Can you come to school with _____ ?

4. Mother will not put the cat _____ in the rain.

5. We can play ball _____ you get here.

Directions: Tell the children, "Read the words in dark print. Then read the incomplete sentences. Find the word in dark print that correctly completes each sentence. Then write that word in the blank. Use a capital letter at the beginning of a sentence."

Dolch **Sight Word Activities**

Name _____

PARENTS: Listen to your child read the sentences on this page and put a check mark beside each sentence that is read without error. Then display the paper in a prominent place. If your child has difficulty with any sentence, read the sentence to the child, pointing to each word as you read. Ask the child to read the sentence in the same way. Repeat this procedure several times.

☐ After you get here,
we will go out and
play together.

☐ Come out of the rain
and sit over here.

☐ Our mother and father
are here with us.

☐ All of us will come
out here after school.

☐ Father will get the big
book out for us to look at.

☐ Do all of you know how
to look after a monkey?

Directions: Tell the children, "Learn to read the sentences, then take them home to read to your parents."

Dalch Sight Word Activities

Name _____

Directions: Tell the children, "Read each sentence below. Say the new word printed in dark print. Then say its letters. Repeat the word. Now trace the word with your pencil."

Did you **thank** the boy for the saw?

thank

I know the boy **from** school.

from

Can you see **what** is under the book?

what

Did he take the little cat to **her**?

her

We will **take** this up to the house.

take

Dolch Sight Word Activities

Name _____

Directions: Tell the children, "Draw a line from each word that begins with a capital letter to the same word that begins with a small letter."

Thank

What

From

Her

Take

from

her

thank

take

what

Take your father
to get a little
cat for us.

You can take a
book out to read.

Directions: Tell the children, "Read each sentence. Draw a picture that shows what the sentence means."

Dolch Sight Word Activities

Name _____

thank _____

what _____

from _____

her _____

take _____

a	a	a	e	e	f	h	h	h	k	k
m	n	o	r	r	t	t	t	w		

Directions: Tell the children, "Copy each of the words on the line next to the word."

Optional Activity: Tell the children, "Cut out the letters at the bottom of the page. Use the letters to make the words. Then glue each word on the line beside the printed word."

Dolch **Sight Word Activities**

Name _____

thank

tha _____

_____ ank

what

_____ ha _____

w _____ t

from

_____ om

fr _____

her

_____ r

h _____

take

_____ ke

ta _____

Dolch Sight Word Activities

Name _____

her
take
from
what
thank

1. _____ _____ the book to school.

2. _____ will you bring us?

3. I can get the book _____ _____ Father.

4. The boy will _____ her for the little puppy.

5. Did you see _____ cat today?

Directions: Tell the children, "Read the words in dark print. Then read the incomplete sentences. Find the word in dark print that correctly completes each sentence. Then write that word in the blank. Use a capital letter at the beginning of a sentence."

Dolch Sight Word Activities

Name _____

PARENTS: Listen to your child read the sentences on this page and put a check mark beside each sentence that is read without error. Then display the paper in a prominent place. If your child has difficulty with any sentence, read the sentence to the child, pointing to each word as you read. Ask the child to read the sentence in the same way. Repeat this procedure several times.

☐ He will take her book to school for her after all.

☐ This big brown chair is from our house.

☐ What is this?

☐ The little girl went from house to house to find her puppy.

☐ Thank you for this funny book.

☐ What will you take with you to school today?

Directions: Tell the children, "Learn to read the sentences, then take them home to read to your parents."

Dolch Sight Word Activities

Unit 19

Letter Tracing 1

Name _____

Directions: Tell the children, "Read the word that goes with each picture. Then say its letters. Repeat the word. Now trace the word with your pencil."

Directions: Tell the children, "Read each sentence below. Say the new word printed in dark print. Then say its letters. Repeat the word. Now trace the word with your pencil."

What is this book **about**?

a͡bout

You can **ride** in the bus with us.

ride

Will you **let** her keep the cat?

let

bus

bus

eat

eat

Dolch Sight Word Activities

Name _____

Directions: Tell the children, "Draw a line from each word that begins with a capital letter to the same word that begins with a small letter."

About	eat
Ride	bus
Bus	let
Eat	about
Let	ride

We can ride
the bus.

We will eat
at school.

Directions: Tell the children, "Read each sentence. Draw a picture that shows what the sentence means."

Dolch **Sight Word Activities**

Name _____

_____

_____ bus

_____

_____ ride

let _____

eat _____

about _____

a	a	b	b	d	e	e	i
l	o	r	s	t	t	t	u

Directions: Tell the children, "Copy each of the words on the line next to the word."

Optional Activity: Tell the children, "Cut out the letters at the bottom of the page. Use the letters to make the words. Then glue each word on the line beside the printed word."

Dolch Sight Word Activities

Name _____

about

ab __ __ t

__ __ out

ride

r __ __ e

__ id __

bus

__ __ s

b __ __

let

__ __ t

l __ __

eat

__ __ t

e __ __

Directions: Tell the children, "Say each word printed in dark type. Fill in the missing letters."

Dolch **Sight Word Activities**

Name _____

about
bus
let
eat
ride

1. The little brown _____ can go fast.

2. Does the girl like to _____ over here?

3. I will _____ the bus to school after I eat.

4. What do you know _____ the little boy?

5. Today mother will _____ me get a monkey.

Directions: Tell the children, "Read the words in dark print. Then read the incomplete sentences. Find the word in dark print that correctly completes each sentence. Then write that word in the blank."

Dalch **Sight Word Activities**

Name _____

PARENTS: Listen to your child read the sentences on this page and put a check mark beside each sentence that is read without error. Then display the paper in a prominent place. If your child has difficulty with any sentence, read the sentence to the child, pointing to each word as you read. Ask the child to read the sentence in the same way. Repeat this procedure several times.

☐ Can we ride the bus to school from here?

☐ What can you find out about this brown cat?

☐ Will your mother let you ride the bus?

☐ Today her puppy will eat at my house.

☐ Father will take the bus to see us play ball.

☐ Take the girl for a bus ride after the rain.

Directions: Tell the children, "Learn to read the sentences, then take them home to read to your parents."

Dalch Sight Word Activities

Name _____

Directions: Tell the children, "Read each sentence below. Say the new word printed in dark print. Then say its letters. Repeat the word. Now trace the word with your pencil."

Get the brown book, **please.**

please

How **much** did you eat?

much

Can you **tell** us what you saw?

tell

What is **that?**

that

Directions: Tell the children, "Read the word that goes with the picture. Then say its letters. Repeat the word. Now trace the word with your pencil."

stop

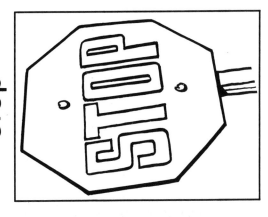

stop

Dolch **Sight Word Activities**

Name _____

Directions: Tell the children, "Draw a line from each word that begins with a capital letter to the same word that begins with a small letter."

Tell

Please

Stop

Much

That

that

much

tell

please

stop

Tell your mother how much you like her.

Tell the little girl to stop that puppy!

Directions: Tell the children, "Read each sentence. Draw a picture that shows what the sentence means."

Dolch Sight Word Activities

Name _____

_____

tell

_____

that

_____

much

_____

please

_____

stop

a	a	c	e	e	e	h	h	l	l
m	o	p	p	s	s	t	t	t	u

Directions: Tell the children, "Copy each of the words on the line next to the word."

Optional Activity: Tell the children, "Cut out the letters at the bottom of the page. Use the letters to make the words. Then glue each word on the line beside the printed word."

Dolch **Sight Word Activities**

Name _____

tell

te____ ____ll

please

pl____se ____ease

stop

____ ____to s____p

much

____ch mu____

that

th____ ____at

Dolch **Sight Word Activities**

Name _____

please
tell
that
stop
much

1. The bus will not _____ _____ here today.

2. How _____ is that brown ball, please?

3. _____ tell the boy where the puppy is.

4. Please put _____ big cat out to run in the grass.

5. Can you _____ me where your mother is?

Directions: Tell the children, "Read the words in dark print. Then read the incomplete sentences. Find the word in dark print that correctly completes each sentence. Then write that word in the blank. Use a capital letter at the beginning of a sentence."

Dolch **Sight Word Activities**

Name _____

PARENTS: Listen to your child read the sentences on this page and put a check mark beside each sentence that is read without error. Then display the paper in a prominent place. If your child has difficulty with any sentence, read the sentence to the child, pointing to each word as you read. Ask the child to read the sentence in the same way. Repeat this procedure several times.

☐ Please tell your
father to bring the
brown book to school.

☐ How much will that
little white cat eat?

☐ Does that bus
stop here?

☐ Please thank the
little girl. She read
that book to me.

☐ Tell the boy to cut the
grass over here, please.

☐ That bus will stop to let
us get out at the school.

Directions: Tell the children, "Learn to read the sentences, then take them home to read to your parents."

Dolch **Sight Word Activities**

Name _____

Directions: Tell the children, "Read the word that goes with each picture. Then say its letters. Repeat the word. Now trace the word with your pencil."

Directions: Tell the children, "Read each sentence below. Say the new word printed in dark print. Then say its letters. Repeat the word. Now trace the word with your pencil."

Do not run **around** in the rain.

around

Did you **ask** the girl to come with us?

ask

My father is **kind.**

kind

write

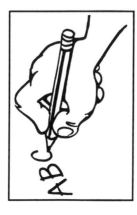

write

light

light

Dalch **Sight Word Activities**

Name _____

Write

Light

Around

Ask

Kind

light

kind

write

around

ask

The boy and girl went around the school.

You can sit here and write to your mother.

Directions: Tell the children, "Read each sentence. Draw a picture that shows what the sentence means."

Dolch **Sight Word Activities**

Name _____

_____ kind

_____ around

_____ write

_____ light

_____ ask

a	a	d	d	e	g	h	i	i	i	k	k	l
n	n	o	r	r	s	t	t	u	w			

Directions: Tell the children, "Copy each of the words on the line next to the word."

Optional Activity: Tell the children, "Cut out the letters at the bottom of the page. Use the letters to make the words. Then glue each word on the line beside the printed word."

Name _____

write

_____ _ ite

wr _____ e

light

li _____ t

_____ ght

around

ar _____ nd

_____ ound

kind

_____ in _____

k _____ d

ask

_____ _ k

s _____

Directions: Tell the children, "Say each word printed in dark type. Fill in the missing letters."

Dolch **Sight Word Activities**

Name _____

ask
around
light
write
kind

1. Can you _ _ _ _ _ _ _ _ _ _ _ _ ?

2. The _ _ _ _ _ _ _ _ _ is on.

3. Is your father _ _ _ _ _ _ _ _ ?

4. The boy is _ _ _ _ _ _ _ _ to the little cat.

5. _ _ _ _ _ _ _ _ the girl and her puppy to come out to play.

Directions: Tell the children, "Read the words in dark print. Then read the incomplete sentences. Find the word in dark print that correctly completes each sentence. Then write that word in the blank. Use a capital letter at the beginning of a sentence."

Dolch **Sight Word Activities**

Name _____

PARENTS: Listen to your child read the sentences on this page and put a check mark beside each sentence that is read without error. Then display the paper in a prominent place. If your child has difficulty with any sentence, read the sentence to the child, pointing to each word as you read. Ask the child to read the sentence in the same way. Repeat this procedure several times.

☐ Ask the kind little girl
to play with the monkey.

☐ I know it will get
light after the rain.

☐ Mother will ask us
to write a play together.

☐ Please put the
light out!

☐ Ask her to take Mother
around the school.

☐ Please write to the girl
and ask her to come to
see me.

Directions: Tell the children, "Learn to read the sentences, then take them home to read to your parents."

Dolch Sight Word Activities

Name _____

Directions Tell the children, "Read each sentence below. Say the new word printed in dark print. Then say its letters. Repeat the word. Now trace the word with your pencil."

What kind **of** puppy is this?

of

Please go to **sleep**.

sleep

You can **help** your mother around the house.

help

He had **no** ball to play with.

no

Ask **him** to ride to school with you.

him

Dalch **Sight Word Activities**

Name _____

Directions: Tell the children, "Draw a line from each word that begins with a capital letter to the same word that begins with a small letter."

Of	no
Sleep	help
Help	him
Him	of
No	sleep

You can help
Father cut grass.

A little cat can
sleep in a big chair.

Directions: Tell the children, "Read each sentence. Draw a picture that shows what the sentence means."

Dalch **Sight Word Activities**

Name _____

_____

sleep _____

no _____

_____

help _____

him _____

_____

of _____

e	e	e	f	h	h	i	l	l
m	n	o	p	p	o	s		

Directions: Tell the children, "Copy each of the words on the line next to the word."

Optional Activity: Tell the children, "Cut out the letters at the bottom of the page. Use the letters to make the words. Then glue each word on the line beside the printed word."

Dalch **Sight Word Activities**

Name _____

help

_ _el_

h_ _p

sleep

_eep

sl_ _p

of

no

him

_ _m

h_

Directions: Tell the children, "Say each word printed in dark type. Fill in the missing letters."

Dolch **Sight Word Activities**

Name _____

help
sleep
him
no
of

1. _____, a cat can not sing.

2. I will tell _____ about my book.

3. My father can _____ in that chair.

4. You can _____ your mother after school.

5. What kind _____ book do you like?

Directions: Tell the children, "Read the words in dark print. Then read the incomplete sentences. Find the word in dark print that correctly completes each sentence. Then write that word in the blank. Use a capital letter at the beginning of a sentence."

Dolch **Sight Word Activities**

Name _____

PARENTS: Listen to your child read the sentences on this page and put a check mark beside each sentence that is read without error. Then display the paper in a prominent place. If your child has difficulty with any sentence, read the sentence to the child, pointing to each word as you read. Ask the child to read the sentence in the same way. Repeat this procedure several times.

☐ My cat can sleep
in the chair.

☐ No, you can not help
him look.

☐ You can sing, and it will
help him go to sleep.

☐ Please let go
of my ball!

☐ Did you ask him
to write to you?

☐ No, the puppy can not
sleep with you.

Directions: Tell the children, "Learn to read the sentences, then take them home to read to your parents."

Dolch **Sight Word Activities**

Name _____

Directions: Tell the children, "Read each sentence below. Say the new words printed in dark print. Then say its letters. Repeat the word. Then trace the word with your pencil."

The light will come on over **there.**   there

We **have** a funny little monkey.   have

Can **some** of you sing?   some

"Come in," **said** Father.   said

Can you get here **if** you take the bus?   if

Dolch **Sight Word Activities**

Name _____

Directions: Tell the children, "Draw a line from each word that begins with a capital letter to the same word that begins with a small letter."

There	said
Have	there
Some	if
If	have
Said	some

There is our big white cat!

Some of us will ride on a bus.

Directions: Tell the children, "Read each sentence. Draw a picture that shows what the sentence means."

Dalch Sight Word Activities

Name _____

_____

there

_____

have

_____

some

_____

if

_____

said

a	a	d	e	e	e	e	f	h	h	i
i	i	m	o	r	s	s	t	v		

Directions: Tell the children, "Copy each of the words on the line next to the word."

Optional Activity: Tell the children, "Cut out the letters at the bottom of the page. Use the letters to make the words. Then glue each word on the line beside the printed word."

Dolch Sight Word Activities

Name _____

some

__ __ __ __

th __ __ me

__ __ so

have

__ __ __ __

ha __ ve

there

__ __ __ __ __

th __ r __ ere

said

__ __ __ __

sa __ id

if

__ __

Dolch Sight Word Activities

Name _____

said
if
some
have
there

1. Do you _____ a brown cat?

2. _____ of you can read this book.

3. _____ he has a ball, we can play with it.

4. "Get out of there!" _____ the girl to the little monkey.

5. "_____ is our bus!" said the little girl to Mother.

Directions: Tell the children, "Read the words in dark print. Then read the incomplete sentences. Find the word in dark print that correctly completes each sentence. Then write that word in the blank. Use a capital letter at the beginning of a sentence."

Dolch **Sight Word Activities**

Name _____

PARENTS: Listen to your child read the sentences on this page and put a check mark beside each sentence that is read without error. Then display the paper in a prominent place. If your child has difficulty with any sentence, read the sentence to the child, pointing to each word as you read. Ask the child to read the sentence in the same way. Repeat this procedure several times.

"Some of you will come to see me in the play," said the boy.

Ask him if there is a bus stop out here.

"I have a little brown puppy for you if you like," said the girl.

There is a funny book about a white cat over there.

The girl and boy have to go to help put on a play.

Did you know that there is a big cat in the grass around the school?

Directions: Tell the children, "Learn to read the sentences, then take them home to read to your parents."

Dolch **Sight Word Activities**

Name _____

Directions: Tell the children, "Read the word that goes with each picture. Then say its letters. Repeat the word. Now trace the word with your pencil."

Directions: Tell the children, "Read each sentence below. Say the new word printed in dark print. Then say its letters. Repeat the word. Now trace the word with your pencil."

What do you **think** about the play?

think

Eat **before** you go to school.

before

The girl is **going** to help Mother.

going

cold

cold

hot

hot

Dolch **Sight Word Activities**

Name _____

Directions: Tell the children, "Draw a line from each word that begins with a capital letter to the same word that begins with a small letter."

Think

Before

Going

Cold

Hot

cold

hot

before

think

going

The boy is going
to play ball.

The girl is going
to play out in
the cold.

Directions: Tell the children, "Read each sentence. Draw a picture that shows what the sentence means."

Dolch **Sight Word Activities**

Name _____

think _____

before _____

cold _____

hot _____

going _____

b	c	d	e	e	f	g	g	h	h	i	i	k
l	l	n	n	o	o	o	o	r	t	t		

Directions: Tell the children, "Copy each of the words on the line next to the word."

Optional Activity: Tell the children, "Cut out the letters at the bottom of the page. Use the letters to make the words. Then glue each word on the line beside the printed word."

Name _____

think

_ h _ nk

thi _ _

before

_ _ fore

be _ re

going

goi _ _

_ _ ing

hot

_ o _

_ _ _ t

cold

_ _ _ ld

co _ _

Directions: Tell the children, "Say each word printed in dark type. Fill in the missing letters."

Name _____

think
before
going
cold
hot

1. It is _____ out today.

2. Are you _____ to school?

3. If I run and jump around, I get _____ .

4. I _____ that I will sing to you.

5. We will eat _____ we come to your house.

Directions: Tell the children, "Read the words in dark print. Then read the incomplete sentences. Find the word in dark print that correctly completes each sentence. Then write that word in the blank."

Dalch **Sight Word Activities**

Name _____

PARENTS: Listen to your child read the sentences on this page and put a check mark beside each sentence that is read without error. Then display the paper in a prominent place. If your child has difficulty with any sentence, read the sentence to the child, pointing to each word as you read. Ask the child to read the sentence in the same way. Repeat this procedure several times.

☐ What do you like to
think about before
going to sleep?

☐ "You will get a cold out
in the rain," said Mother.

☐ Father is going to write
to you if you write to him.

☐ I think he is going
to stop over there
to ask for some help.

☐ Do you think it is going
to get hot or cold today?

☐ Think if it is hot or cold
before going out.

Directions: Tell the children, "Learn to read the sentences, then take them home to read to your parents."

Dolch Sight Word Activities

Name _____

Directions: Tell the children, "Read each sentence below. Say the new word printed in dark print. Then say its letters. Repeat the word. Now trace the word with your pencil."

I **am** not a funny monkey.   **am**

The puppy is going to play with **its** ball.   **its**

He **would** like to get up before it is light.   **would**

You **may** have the puppy if you like.   **may**

I **found** a little cat on the bus.   **found**

Name _____

Directions: Tell the children, "Draw a line from each word that begins with a capital letter to the same word that begins with a small letter."

Am

Its

Would

May

Found

would

found

am

its

may

I am with
my father.

The girl found
a big brown cat.

Directions: Tell the children, "Read each sentence. Draw a picture that shows what the sentence means."

Dalch **Sight Word Activities**

Name _____

_____

am _____

would _____

_____

may _____

found _____

_____

its _____

a	a	d	d	f	i	l	l	m	m
n	o	o	s	u	u	t	w	y	

Directions: Tell the children, "Copy each of the words on the line next to the word."

Optional Activity: Tell the children, "Cut out the letters at the bottom of the page. Use the letters to make the words. Then glue each word on the line beside the printed word."

Dolch **Sight Word Activities**

Name _____

would

w _____ _____ l d

_____ o u _____ d

its

_____ _____ s

i _____ _____

am

_____ _____ _____ _____

found

f _____ _____ n d

f o u _____ _____

may

m _____ _____ y

Directions: Tell the children, "Say each word printed in dark type. Fill in the missing letters."

Dolch Sight Word Activities

Name _____

found

may

would

its

am

1. I _____ not your mother.

2. _____ I take you out to eat?

3. _____ you like to play at our house?

4. We _____ my little book under the chair.

5. I think I know where your cat put _____ ball.

Directions: Tell the children, "Read the words in dark print. Then read the incomplete sentences. Find the word in dark print that correctly completes each sentence. Then write that word in the blank. Use a capital letter at the beginning of a sentence."

Dolch **Sight Word Activities**

Name _____

PARENTS: Listen to your child read the sentences on this page and put a check mark beside each sentence that is read without error. Then display the paper in a prominent place. If your child has difficulty with any sentence, read the sentence to the child, pointing to each word as you read. Ask the child to read the sentence in the same way. Repeat this procedure several times.

☐ Would all of you like to write in my book?

☐ The girl found my cat over there.

☐ Father may have found the bus stop after all.

☐ I am going to stop going to school in May.

☐ If you found a monkey, would you take it to see your mother?

☐ The puppy found its ball in the grass.

Directions: Tell the children, "Learn to read the sentences, then take them home to read to your parents."

Answer Key

Dolch **Sight Word Activities** Volume 1

Unit 1, Lesson 5

1. a
2. read
3. can
4. boy *or* girl
5. boy *or* girl

Unit 2, Lesson 5

1. cat *or* puppy
2. sing
3. book
4. not
5. cat *or* puppy

Unit 3, Lesson 5

1. laugh
2. had
3. and
4. laugh *or* run *or* jump
5. laugh *or* run *or* jump

Unit 4, Lesson 5

1. Is
2. The
3. fast
4. funny
5. with

Unit 5, Lesson 5

1. school
2. chair *or* grass *or* school *or* rain
3. chair *or* grass *or* school *or* rain
4. chair *or* grass *or* school *or* rain
5. in

Unit 6, Lesson 5

1. Will
2. at
3. sit
4. to
5. on

Unit 7, Lesson 5

1. ball
2. I
3. brown
4. go *or* play
5. go

Unit 8, Lesson 5

1. house
2. Today
3. little
4. look
5. saw

Unit 9, Lesson 5

1. Does
2. white
3. it
4. monkey
5. are

Unit 10, Lesson 5

1. Bring
2. keep *or* bring
3. like
4. he
5. for

Unit 11, Lesson 5

1. Come
2. She
3. me
4. see
5. my

Unit 12, Lesson 5

1. under
2. Where
3. find
4. you
5. Put *or* Find

Unit 13, Lesson 5

1. has
2. together
3. Did
4. big
5. Yes

Unit 14, Lesson 5

1. mother
2. went
3. your
4. over
5. know

Unit 15, Lesson 5

1. How
2. We
3. Do
4. was
5. Father

Unit 16, Lesson 5

1. cut
2. up
3. our *or* this
4. this
5. Get

Unit 17, Lesson 5

1. Here
2. all
3. us
4. out
5. after

Unit 18, Lesson 5

1. Take
2. What
3. from
4. thank
5. her

Unit 19, Lesson 5

1. bus
2. ride *or* eat
3. ride
4. about
5. let

Unit 20, Lesson 5

1. stop
2. much
3. Please
4. that
5. tell

Unit 21, Lesson 5

1. write *or* ask
2. light
3. around *or* kind
4. kind
5. Ask

Unit 22, Lesson 5

1. No
2. him
3. sleep
4. help
5. of

Unit 23, Lesson 5

1. have
2. Some
3. If
4. said
5. There

Unit 24, Lesson 5

1. cold *or* hot
2. going
3. hot
4. think
5. before

Unit 25, Lesson 5

1. am
2. May
3. Would
4. found
5. its

NOTES

NOTES

NOTES

NOTES